Four Dots

Keep a close eye out for those dots in sets of four because that means there are a million more words that could be said, but the poem could not fit anymore....

kerr mc

India | USA | UK

Copyright © kerr mc
All Rights Reserved.

This book has been self-published with all reasonable efforts taken to make the material error-free by the author. No part of this book shall be used, reproduced in any manner whatsoever without written permission from the author, except in the case of brief quotations embodied in critical articles and reviews.

The Author of this book is solely responsible and liable for its content including but not limited to the views, representations, descriptions, statements, information, opinions, and references ["Content"]. The Content of this book shall not constitute or be construed or deemed to reflect the opinion or expression of the Publisher or Editor. Neither the Publisher nor Editor endorse or approve the Content of this book or guarantee the reliability, accuracy, or completeness of the Content published herein and do not make any representations or warranties of any kind, express or implied, including but not limited to the implied warranties of merchantability, fitness for a particular purpose.

The Publisher and Editor shall not be liable whatsoever...

Made with ❤ on the BookLeaf Publishing Platform
www.bookleafpub.in
www.bookleafpub.com

Dedication

Dedicated to you....
Because these poems would still be swirling in my head,
with no one to read them,
and with no muse....

Preface

Four dots....

Because of all the unspoken things that can't fit into the ominous three.

Because it's too complicated to say "I love you."

Because of all the silent tears staining these pages.

Because saying "I miss you" can't cover the depth of missing.

Because anger can't be spoken aloud sometimes.

Because there are still a million coffee cups to share, and a thousand conversations we've yet to have.

Four dots, because there is more silence than could ever fit into three.

Acknowledgements

Keep a close eye out for those dots in sets of four,
because that means there are a million more words that could be said,
but the poem could not fit anymore....
So let's save the rest for coffee and long conversations,
where the pauses speak louder than the words ever could....

I. coffee says "I love you...."

I Say "I love you,"
With a cup of coffee—
Or tea, if you prefer?
But I'd love it if you had it with me;
We can sit, as our cups we stir.

We don't always have to go to a café;
The front porch will do.
We can sit in our rocking chairs
And talk—and for that moment, have nothing but me and you.

It can be a rushed coffee,
A quick Sunday morning brew,
But I'll smile when I see you take a sip—
The same old mug greeting a day, making it new.

It can be over the phone,
After you've had a long night.
I'll just send you seven bucks,
And say, "Oat milk latte on me." I hope it makes you feel bright.

We can climb up on the roof,

Our cups warming our hands.
No words need to be said—
Just watch our shadows slowly move across the grass-covered land.

I'll buy you one for weeks after I see you cry,
Because a hug and words can't always stop the tears.
But I'll remember your order, and we'll sing to your favorite playlist
While you overcome your fears.

I say "I love you,"
In one sugar or two?
Coffee always seems to lead to conversations—
A million conversations I want to have with you.

We could sit at the table, the window our view,
And get so caught up in words
Our coffee goes cold—your tea does too.

The world is busy,
We all have so many plans.
So let me buy you a coffee—
A small, warm hug in the palm of your hands.

Let's drink coffee in the rain,
And sing out our favorite song.

Who cares if we catch a cold,
Or if we get all the words wrong?

I've memorized your order,
And I pin it up with your laugh.
I say "I love you" in a cup,
Or in a bookshop we happen to pass.

Fill the sink with mugs,
Fill the cupboard with beans,
Because we have many mornings ahead—
Stains on the table are valuable, so it may seem.

They say home isn't a place,
But the people who find you when you feel alone.
I believe that is true—
Because I do not have a place,
But my, I have so many homes.

People say I'm addicted,
Always at a café or making a new brew.
But I'm truly addicted to something else—
The smile that coffee always brings to you.

Coffee says, "I love you."
Tea says, "It's true."

So with my car keys in my hand I'll say,
"I'm going out for coffee—can I get one for you?"

II. sincerely, jack

My name is jack
Because no other suits me right.
I have done a lot of things
But never master the trade before I leave the town in the dead of night

When I was young I knew
Just what I wanted to be
But as a grew older
I realized I hadn't thought about other possibilities

I've come to a age now
Where I don't even want to choose
I want to dip my fingers into a million paints
And see what my canvas will brew

I have those wonderful nights
When my head is my home
And I have those awful nights
When my head won't let me go.

I have those blissful days
That I want never to end
I have those long days

That I just want to curl up in my bed.

I have many a friends
Or so if may seem
But I truly have a chose few
Who always catch me when I begin to lean

I have many plans
Much inspiration and gleam
I don't tell people I would be content
If I could have my one true dream.

A dream to be one thing
And that thing can't be defined
Like the space in a notebook
Right between the black lines

I want to be the moon
The one that shines in the day
I want to be a random person
Who goes on a walk but only when it rains

I want to be a person
who is okay to hurt
One who can seem overly optimistic
But does sincerely love to work.

I want to be invisible
Unimportant to the everyday life
So that the world doesn't care
And I can venture into the everyday night....

I want to not make sense
Because I speak crazy beautiful things
Who needs to talk about sad things
When there are wildflowers in the spring

But i won't mind sad things
No not at all
Sad things will give me inspiration
Keep me smiling through it all.

I could be a writer,
A poet,
A painter,
A pen,

A hiker
A actor
A lover
Or just a simple friend.

I could be rich
I'd rather be poor.

No matter what I am
I will love with the heart of an open door.

And when people ask me my name
I will say my name is jack
Because I've been in many trades
But it's only mastering I lack

I dont know if I'll be okay
I dont know who ill marry and love
But I know I love this chaotic life
And if that is my only mastering that is enough

III. the Fall

If a leaf never fell
It would lose its purpose to grow
Because falling gives life meaning
And without it we miss the privilege to know.

Know what you may ask?
well, listen close and let me tell...
if the leaf never grew
it would never have fell.

It would've never seen the view
 from the top of the trees,
the sunsets that came
-even if there was no one else around to see.

It would have never seen the spring come
or taste the summer rain.
and sure, it faced some storms- but the sunny days still came.

And in the end,
when winter had once again come
its life changed completely
when it became the color of the sun.

When its last days came
it shorn brightest of all
and it took one final glance
of its life up so tall.

As it fell to the ground,
it finally knew:
that falling was only part of the reason
it had the pleasure to bloom.

IV. hide and seek

There's still something out there
Something begging to be found
I don't know if it's calling from the sky
Or if it's here on the damp ground.

I've looked for it everywhere,
From sea to sea
But I still haven't found it
And it's forever calling to me.

It's so close to my heart
A void that beckons to be filled
But it's so far away
It whispers to me from beyond the hills.

I tried the jungles far away
And the states so near
I tried the land of fairytales
And I tried writing it on paper, but it would tear.

It beckons to be found
I hear it in the rain
I hear it in the river
It knows my name.

It wants to be found
But it wants to be chased
And it knows I don't mind the venture
It knows I will keep running the race.

It comes to me at night
Or when I read a good book
It reminds me of its presence
When it seems I've given up.

It won't tell me its name
So I have nothing to say when people ask what I search
And it laughs when I shrug my shoulders
And when I complain my feet hurt.

Venture after venture
Plane after plane
I keep looking for it
I keep asking its name.

I've gotten used to the ache now
It's not so desperate a plea
Until it taps me once again
And says, "There's something you must see."

It comes to me with friends

With my family when we laugh
It comes when the wind
Tickles the tops of the grass.

The sweet taste of an adventure
The one which addicts me so
It comes to me when it pleases
Constant to come and go.

I think I'm the only one who can hear it
That's why to me it frequently calls
So even though I've only just begun to rest
I get up again
Even with the possibility I will fall.

Others have searched with me
Sometimes I go alone
But one day I'll find it
And then I think I will finally find my hom

V. a pirate, a sap, and a tree

I started out without a cause
I was a pirate on the mighty sea
Not bothering with laws.

I was a sly young sap with a spring in my step
But I just went in circles whenever I would skip.

I was a lonely old tree
Who stood high and tall
But with no leaves on my branches
It seemed I had no life at all.

Then you came along at the most unexpected of times
And you gave me a new verse to my song, you finished my rhyme.

You took my pirate ship and settled on my deck
And flew up to the crow's nest high.
You said, "Land ho!"
Though that island wasn't in my plan, that was the best stop yet.

You took my skipping feet and turned them into a dance
And we danced all night,

Your hands in my hands.

You took my empty branches and made them your home
—
A treehouse of love,
A place for joy to grow.

So you see, without you,
I just wouldn't be me.
I would be a pirate with no ship,
A sap with no step,
A tree with no leaves.

So I beg you to stay,
For if you ever left
I would have no place to go
Except to the place where we first met.

VI. i want to cry....

Want to Cry...

I want to cry,
Watching you go.
I felt so brave with you here,
Now I just feel alone.

I want to cry.
Our time went much too fast.
We became a very close team;
Unfortunately, the world is very vast.

I want to cry
Because my tears win over being strong.
My smile broke
As I listened to all our songs.

I want to cry
Because I'm sitting in these hard pews without my team —

A brother's arm on my back
And a friend that kept us laughing.

I want to cry

Because they believe I'm strong.
But I know I'm not—
A flower in the wild,
But so much safer in a pot.

I want to cry
Because I'm selfish,
Begging them to stay in my little life.
Days so much sweeter with them,
And easier were the sleepless nights.

I want to cry
Because I'm lost,
Though I know exactly where I am.
What's the point in having a map
If you have no destination planned?

I want to cry
Because I accidentally let them see me cry.
I wanted them to see me okay.
I wanted to say "see you later" instead of goodbye.

I want to cry
Because I want to be with them.
Our lives are the same—
Only, separated by two continents.

I want to cry
Because I have to pretend I'm okay.
Keep smiling for the crowds,
Hide my fear by shaking my legs.

I want to cry.
I did.
Now I'm saying "I'm fine,"
Halfway through this chapter,
Just finishing one day at a time.

I want to cry
Because they don't need me to be okay.
But we needed each other's laughs
To fulfill our long days.

I want to cry
But instead I cover my face.
I want them to know I'll miss them
Sharing my life's space.

I want to cry
But I hold up my hands in the shape of a heart.
This is just the ending of a chapter
Before the next one can start.

VII. stop lights

As a girl, I remember sitting in my Popop's truck.
"How do you pray?"
I would ask.
And my grandma would start to explain...

"You pray by saying 'Dear Jesus,' and end by saying
'Amen.'
But you always thank God first. Then, 'Grandma,
Grandpa, Mawmaw, Pawpaw, aunts, uncles, and cousins.'

You pray for those hurting, and ask for help if you need,
And you end with 'I love you, Jesus,' then get up off your
knees."

I looked out the window of that big white truck,
And I saw an ambulance going right past us.

I prayed that the doctor would be able to help those
people,
And that they would be all right.
Then I looked up and thanked God for the stoplights.

As I grew up, I began to pray more.
I prayed for relief of pain, and that the Lord would show

us His plan in store.
I pray for healing, and I pray for peace.
I pray for His coming—that someday soon it will be.

I pray for a family who just lost their son.
I pray for a mother whose child's life hadn't even begun.

I pray for surgeries, and for travels to go well.
I pray for presidents—that truth would always be what we tell.

Such adultish prayers that make so much sense.
But some days I miss those learning prayer days,
When I would just talk to Jesus about my new dress.

And as I grow, with my prayer list in my sight,
I may lose my childish wishes,
But I still pray for the ambulances and the fire trucks,
And sometimes I still thank Jesus for the stoplights....

VIII. memory

It astounds me sometimes how the senses can hold so much—
How memories come flooding back through taste, smell, and touch.
Sometimes I welcome it; sometimes it aches.
But now that I know it can happen, I stay awake—alert for when it breaks.

"How does it work?" you might ask—I truly don't know.
It's the good and the bad—
The holding on,
And the letting go.

I smell frozen pizza, and I'm swept away
To a rollerblading rink on some forgotten day.
You were there—laughing at our clumsy parade,
At me falling into you,
Afraid you'd be mad—
But you only smiled,
And let out a soft laugh.

I was on top of the world, spinning round and around,
In the glow of the disco, true joy I'd found.

I smell fire and imagine a warm, gentle glow,
And I'm taken back to a cold night—
You across from me,
Laughing through the smoke of burnt marshmallow.

I remember songs,
And the whisper of a prayer—
A cool breeze that carried a goodbye through the air.
The faint scent of smoke,
A tear in my eye—
The ache of a moment that refused to die.

Is that sand I smell, and the tint of salt?
I close my eyes, hear the waves exalt,
And laugh again at your seagull cry—
Your wings of silliness across the sky.

I feel the sand beneath my nails,
When we wrote our creed in the shore's soft hand:
Love equals insanity—and together we stand.

I'll never forget those smiles, those laughs,
The songs we sang too loud on the way back.
And when I said goodbye, I wished I hadn't so soon—
On the ride home I held in the tears,
Till my phone dinged—
And yours had already bloomed.

So, I gave up on being strong,
And cried because you did too.

The smell of spice takes me to a jungle, hot and green,
Where we sang *Hakuna Matata* like it meant everything.
Small arms around my waist,
And the smile of a boy who'd just found grace.

I smile now, because if I try hard enough,
I can almost hear your voice—
But I have to listen quick,
Before the blur takes choice.

So, I gather the fragments, the scents, the strands—
The feel of your arms,
The ghost of your hands.
I don't care if they fade, or if people don't understand—
Why I memorize taste, and texture, and sand.

But take this warning,
A truth I've learned:
If you try to control the memory, it's one not earned.
Let them come gently,
Let them go when they must—
For if you cling too tightly,
It becomes one you can't trust.

IX. bloody heart on my sleeve

People always say I wear my heart on my sleeve.
They say I love deeply—too deeply, too fast, too much—
because the people I love will never love me so in return.

Yet I've kept my arms open,
exposed to anyone who needs me to hold them,
even if they bear a knife.
And my sleeve has been bruised, cut, stabbed, and sore.

I see it now—
the grey hairs, the loss of trust,
the tiredness in my eyes—
but still, my arms remain open.

Not because I am better than anyone,
but because I know I am worse.

And in a world of terrible things,
of broken hearts and hidden pain,
I was meant to remain the thing that is open,
the thing people can run to.

I don't want to put up a fence

if it means I block my view of the world.

So, with tears on my cheeks and a bloody sleeve,
I go from a deep love to a stubborn love.

The world is still beautiful,
and things ever change.
But if you need me, I'm here.
Hurt me a million times—
the battered heart on my sleeve will remain.

X. to the baby who stole my breath

Oh little baby,
I got to meet you today—
A blessing I didn't know I'd have,
And yet it was the best part of my day.

As you lay in your mom's arms,
Your beauty took my breath away.
It wasn't like a normal baby...
It was like a ray of sunshine on a cloudy day.

You looked so beautiful,
Like a million new songs—
Like tears and smiles,
And a praise like one of David's psalms.

"Do you want to hold her?"
Your mom asked.
And I thought my heart would melt
As into my arms you were passed.

I tried to play it cool,
But tears began to fill my eyes,
When I realized how much I already loved you,

And I looked into blue like the sky.

Your mom kept talking—
I was at a loss for words,
As I got to hold you close
And enjoy a miracle from the Lord.

I've held so many babies,
And for each of them I care.
But you took my breath away, Selah...
Because I realized I was holding an answered prayer.

Oh, baby girl,
You have no idea how you made my heart smile,
As your mom and I talked
And napped the whole while.

I couldn't put you down...
I didn't want to say goodbye.
You felt like a reminder from Jesus
That the sun is still in the sky.

The prayers I've prayed for you,
Getting to hold you tonight—
I know you're not old enough to understand,
So I figured I needed to write.

This poem is for you, Selah,
Maybe when you're old enough to understand,
How dearly your parents and family love you,
And how Jesus is holding your tiny hand.

Life will have its rain,
And you will cry many tears.
But tonight you gave me a small blessing,
And this poem will hold it for all of my years.

To the dear little baby,
The one that stole away my breath—
I shed my tears for you now,
And I write them down with my pen.

I can't wait to watch you grow up.
You make old faith shine like new.
Keep stealing away everyone's breath
By showing off what the Lord can do.

I witnessed true beauty today,
And I don't say that in vain.
I want this memory to last forever,
And a poem is the best way....

XI. pillows

The pillows on the couch
Miss being thrown,
And the speakers around the house
Are absent of music's tone.

The mugs on the counter—
They miss being filled,
Held in laughter,
Laughter so hard they spilled.

The keys on the desk—
They miss being tossed,
Being left behind
As friends left to get lost.

The van in the drive
Wants to be moved,
Wants its horn to honk—
Not in anger, but like the friends would do.

The sink in the kitchen—
It wants to be filled.
Dishes mean life,
They mean banter

Between friends who can't hold still.

The mountains
Want to be seen,
The backdrop to a picture that says,
"Man, we make a good team."

The dirt roads—
They want to be walked,
In silence or laughter,
Nostalgia never to stop.

My phone wants to be used
For texts that read,
"On our way home,"
That meant I wasn't entirely alone.

The coffee shop
Wants our table to stay ours,
So we can make everyone annoyed
Because we laugh too hard.

The playlists—
They want to grow,
To be full of songs and vibes,
With lyrics our hearts will always know.

The shoes on the porch
Don't want to be by themselves.
They want to be crowded—
With Converse and Crocs,
And Hey Dudes side by side on the shelf.

The girl—
She is tired of being brave.
She wants to take a nap on the couch
And sing Christmas songs at the end of the day.

The airport floors
Want to mop up my tears.
They want to bring me warmth.
They want to tell me not to fear.

The airplane—
It wants to turn around,
To unite the team again
And bring them back to common ground.

The days want to end
So the friends can be together.
No letters have to be sent.
So they catch our tears and whisper,
"Please don't cry. This isn't the end."

So the girl fakes bravery,
And the boys' lives once again start.
But the memories are vivid,
And in a world of worries,
They know their memories will never part.

XII. if it was up to me

If it was up to me,
You'd never have to stop smiling.
I'd walk beside you each step of each day,
Just to hear your laughter rising.

If it was up to me,
I'd erase every bad memory a rainy day held—
Wipe away each tear,
And the reason it ever fell.

If it was up to me,
You'd never have to say goodbye—
That ache that cuts the deepest,
The one that lingers in the sigh.

If it was up to me,
You'd understand the reason for every pain,
And you'd see how good still echoes softly
Even in the rain.

If it was up to me,
I'd take it all away—
The hurt, the loss, the sorrow.
I'd carry it myself,

And I'd do it again tomorrow.

But it's not up to me,
And that's the hardest part—
Not being able to catch you
Every time you fall apart.

But what *is* up to me,
I'll strive each day to do—
To be constant,
And always true.

I can't stop the rain,
But I can hold your hand and dance in puddles.
I can't chase away the dark,
But I can sit beside you and whisper of stars.

I can't promise a life without another goodbye,
But I can hold you close to my heart,
Wish you the sweetest memories,
And remind you—it's good to be alive.

If it was up to me,
You might not be as strong as you are.
So here's my promise to you:
My heart will be with you always—

**Through good and bad,
Near or far.**

XIII. lost

I feel a bit lost these days,
Just walking about,
Like a trail with no loop,
No destination to be found.

I feel like I'm walking in circles,
Or not walking at all.
I'm just existing in a world
Where the story travels on.

I'm floating above,
Neither here nor there.
People think me odd
As they stop and stare.

They ask me my reason,
My purpose and plans.
They ask me if I'm okay
With traveling as a lone man.

I answer them kindly
With a shake of my head.
I tell them honestly I'm lost—
I have no destination to call my bed.

I'm looking thoroughly
For a spark of life,
A fill to the void
That wants to be discovered by light.

I think I find it
In the small things I find—
In the crackle of a fire,
Or in the horse's galloping stride.

But I lose my way again
When the road of life demands to be seen,
And once again I'm lost
With my map of a million streets.

I can see the world better
When I catch the glimpses of fiction.
I can clearly hear the mountains sing,
But I have to get lost and listen.

And when I try to drag others
To the world I have found,
They smile at my stories
And kindly tie my balloon to the ground.

Not all those who wander are lost,

As they say in stories of old.
And I know the meaning
As I shiver from a blissful cold.

I know the meaning
When I cry alone in the woods,
Or when I dance in the rain
Like no grown-up could.

It's okay to be lost,
For you find things never found.
You find that maps hold a lot less on their paper
Than the world holds in ground.

XIV. hold your hand

I love holding your hands—
When I was little and even now.
They hold so many memories,
And confidence they always allow.

I held them when I was small,
My hands big enough to hold only your thumb.
We'd play a game: *who can squeeze the hardest?*
Yeah.... you always won.

I remember all of your callouses
As you taught me to work.
Putting in an outlet isn't right
If your hands can't handle a little dirt.

I remember the scars,
Because you couldn't go a day without some kind of injury.
You'd walk in, telling Grandma not to worry—
She'd put on a Band-Aid, and you'd be working again in a hurry.

I remember the times you held my hand when I cried,
When I couldn't figure out fifth-grade math.

I remember you helping me finish,
And telling me of the fun we'd have.

In church you would hold my hand,
And Grandma would hold your other—
Never letting go
As we prayed at the altar.

Holding hands to pray at dinner,
Holding hands before you tucked us into bed,
Falling asleep laughing from tickles,
And waking up with "Jesus loves me" and "Get up, you bonehead."

You're still holding Grandma's hand,
And still kissing her goodnight—
Showing all of us kids what true love is,
That putting others over self is always right.

Dog kisses on the cheek,
Taking me hunting my first time,
Loving Grandma with all your heart,
Making your family your life.

You're gonna get better soon,
I can feel your hands are still strong.

And you have your family all around you—
For the good days and the long.

XV. a cottage for a castle

A princess lives in the mind of a scullery maid.
She's not much to look at—ordinary as the rest—
But on the inside, she has a heart of gold,
And she doesn't really care what the other princesses say.

She loves the smell of dirt
And likes to feel moss beneath her toes.
But oh, what an improper thing
For a princess who smells of rose.

Her castle is made of trees,
With flowers for her guards.
She loves her family, and she loves them so deeply
They have no need of alarm.

She's satisfied with her life of hard work and pain,
Because one day after another, nothing is the same.
When the day comes that she meets a swine
On her solitary trail,
She doesn't remember feeling anything like it before—
And she didn't think the feeling could go stale.

The boy was as ragged in looks as she,

With mysterious brown eyes
And hands as calloused as can be.

But those calloused hands never let go of hers,
And as the days grew on,
She allowed him to be the prince of her mind.
Those mysterious brown eyes became what she preferred.

When they both came of age,
And time allowed the tie,
The swine boy got on his knee
With a twinkling in his eye.
And the mystery in the brown
Was something she simply had to find.

They didn't spend their honeymoon
In a palace or castle high,
But they spent it in the woods
And made their own kingdom—
With another few sets of brown eyes.

Now that maid and swine boy
Are the richest king and queen of all,
As they watch their tiny army
Grow up and slay dragons tall.

They've grown weary and old,
But their cottage still seems like a castle.
His hands still hold her close each night.
They still sing their love song off-key,
And it still doesn't matter.

Love and respect carry them
Through each and every winter,
And when they both come to the end,
They write with honesty and truth:
"And we lived happily ever after...

XVI. untitled....

Want to know something ridiculous?
I haven't been able to stop thinking of you since I left,
And I replay every moment we've had together—
From the moment we first met.

What's ridiculous is the moment I actually looked into your eyes-
And I wanted so badly to know how those eyes looked when you laughed and when you cried.

Could I wave hello?
Or would that be too much?
Surely you would know
My friendship is a disguised crush.

What's ridiculous
Is the petals that said, "He loves me, he loves me not..."
And me hiding that flower, embarrassed at my smile if I ever was caught.

What's ridiculous
Is the way you help me open up.
You care about my favorite color.
And you make ice skating not seem so tough.

What's ridiculous
Is the way I say, "We're just friends."
Because what a string of lies—
Friends don't change their favorite color
To match the color of your eyes.

Call me ridiculous—
Make it my full name.
Because I can't stop thinking of you
In every moment of every day.

Every love song is about you,
And every single shade of blue.
But I can't look at you while you talk,
And I can't say yes to going on a walk.

A Pinterest board is created with quotes I apply to you,
And I asked all of my friends if they think you feel it too.

The nonsense has escalated—
As ridiculous as it might be,
I hope your mind is full of ridiculous thoughts,
Ridiculous thoughts that are all about me.

But it's okay,
We can just pretend we are sane.

But on the inside—
My, you have made quite the mess of my brain.

Waterfalls say "I love you" now,
And clothespins say, "It's true."
My notebooks keep telling me
They are very tired of being told about you.

Want to know something ridiculous?
You will probably never read these lines.
So in the safety of these pages I say...
"I just want you to be mine."

Could I add another stanza?
Or would that be ridiculous too?
Heavens, if I add any more,
I would make this poem's title *You.*

XVII. Pikes Peak

I climbed a mountain today,
And it stole my breath.
I hadn't trained before the climb,
And my legs quivered with each step.

I could've stayed in the car,
But the rocks beckoned me, "Come."
So I took off my seatbelt
And set out for the peak above.

My calves grew sore,
My lungs stung with the cold air,
But I had to keep going up,
To follow the sun's sharp glare.

I reached a peak
And lost my breath once again.
The red rocks around me bloomed,
And I wished I had brought my paper and pen.

I wanted to describe the flowers—
Purple and vibrant yellow—
Among the harsh green
And vast red of the mountain meadow.

I felt so small,
But fulfilled in the view.
Then something called me again,
Ever up into the sky of blue.

So once again, I climbed,
My bones protesting each step,
Until I reached the next outlook,
And new expectations were met.

The previous view was grand,
But look at this—
My feet dangled from the rock ledge
Into the beautiful vast abyss.

Once again,
The sky said, "Closer still."
So I left the peace I had found
And struggled up the sloped hill.

I climbed and climbed,
Until my breaths and the wind mixed into one,
Until the sky told me the views
Would be my prize to be won.

Grabbing a small stone,

I ascended the final peak,
And the view was before me—
The blue sky and the cliffs deep.

I took my small rock,
Placing it at the top.
I wanted to make that mountain higher,
I wanted the view's growth to never stop.

I sat for a few moments,
My feet over the rocky sides.
I let the wind ruin my hair,
And the sun overwhelm my eyes.

I tried to write it down—
How alone and together I felt—
But words wouldn't come,
For how amazing the wildflowers smelt.

I wished for many things in that moment,
For loved ones to be by my side.
I sent them silent prayers,
Hoping they'd know that on top of the world, they were on my mind.

I wished for the future,
And wished for the past.

I wished for the present
Never to end—oh please, may it last.

But I had to climb down,
My wilting flowers in tow.
I had to come back down to earth,
Leaving the young new flowers to grow.

As I descended from the sky,
I looked back at my castle of rocks,
And I swear I heard the mountains whisper my name and say,
"But you haven't yet seen the top."

I see now—life is like mountains.
It holds a million new sights,
And no matter how far up you go,
You may never reach its highest heights.

It beckons, "Climb."
You never know what's over the next ridge—
A waterfall, an airplane, or a scary, beautiful bridge.

You face the fear of the view,
Then say, "Here I'll stay."
But life says, "I hold more,
Just up this way."

So we climb, we hurt,
We lose our breath.
And just when we're about to say it wasn't worth it,
The mountains justify our steps.

This wasn't the first mountain I climbed,
And it certainly won't be my last.
Just as my life isn't grown from my future—
It grows from my past.

XVIII. i wish....

How can you sum up a life of pure joy in a sentence or two words?
Another year has passed, and I've taken another turn.

I wish I could go back and thank each new friend I met—
Tell them they changed me for good and that they were heaven-sent.

I wish I could hug each loved one closer before I said goodbye.
I wish I would've smiled more, but I didn't know how time would fly.

I wish I would've sat back and taken in each precious day,
Instead of wishing ahead at what may or may not be coming my way.

I wish I would've prayed more so I could know my Saviour dear,
For in my heart, I know now He is the only reason I am here.

"You will wish you would've valued your time more," the

wise used to say,
But I was youthful and so busy in my own way.

Now I wish I'd have listened, because I miss my past—
The days of childish games, the days of easy laughs.

So today, as I grow one more year,
I wish for wisdom; I wish for my family to stay near.

I wish to be an example for all those that come next.
I wish for good memory, and on the good my eyes would fix.

I wish for each of you to grow—happy and strong.
I wish you longing for understanding of our God.

I wish to apologize for any I've done wrong.
I wish you music—that you always have a song.

I wish you the brightest of days, and I pray you know I will never forget:
You changed me for good, and you will always be my friend.

I wish, in the future, that our paths will cross again.
This is my birthday wish....

XIX. feel pretty

You make me feel pretty,
But not by your words.
You silently taught me the language of "pretty"—
It's something I hadn't yet learned.

You make me feel pretty
Because of the way you care,
How you put in hard work
And prove to me you're there.

You make me feel pretty
In all those little things you do—
Challenging me to work harder,
Or carrying my shoes.

The way that you smile,
I think, says it most of all.
You see all of me and still say "beautiful,"
Including all of my flaws.

You don't ignore my shortcomings,
You don't push them under a shelf.
You bring them out in the open
And say, "They just need a little help."

You make me feel beautiful,
Encouraging me to work for my dreams.
The whole world says, "Do better,"
You just join in with me.

I feel so special
When I get to have you here—
Just taking me to coffee,
Or walking with you near.

You listened to my love of sunsets,
You picked me up a fallen leaf.
You changed my whole perspective
Of the boy I thought I'd meet.

You make me feel pretty
Because you like my colorless eyes.
You love my crazy family,
You take us all out for French fries.

You make me happy.
You make me smile.
You make me feel worth it,
Walking a thousand miles.

So I am thankful for you,

Because you taught me "pretty" is more than looks.
You wrote me poetry,
And it was based on my favorite books.

You saw something invisible.
I traded my name for a new friend.
I hope I can pay you back,
So I dedicate all the ink in this pen.

I'm not good with words
When out loud I have them to say.
My notebook is my advocate—
I'll gift it to you one day.

I hope you'll understand,
For you I feel the same.
I too think you're pretty—
Prettier than the sun, because I love the rain.

XX. first snow of the year....

As we drive along this plain November night,
I glance at the sky—and oh, what a sight!

For when I looked up, I expected dark with maybe a few stars,
Instead, I saw tiny bits of white, drifting softly into people's yards.

My smile spreads as my thoughts come to life;
Though I've been wearing the sweaters and listening to the tunes, it hadn't yet felt quite right.

But now! I let the cold bite my nose,
And begin to forget my poor, frosty toes!

It smells of cold, and cinnamon, and new—
And in my heart, I know the holidays are soon due.

So with a smile on my face and a spring in my step,
I glance toward the heavens with a hand outstretched.

I cherish each small flake that falls into my palms,
And the quiet hope that fills me with a Christmas song.

Oh, beautiful world—catch your glimpse quick!
I'm afraid this sacred frost won't have too long to stick.

So I shout to the world with a simple cheer:
"Things are looking up, everyone—
It's the first snow of the year!"

XXI. muse

You can call me a writer
If you think that title fits.
The truth is, I'm not a writer anymore,
Because a muse is what I miss.

See, I used to not need a muse,
Finding inspiration in anything I'd see—
Maybe a yellow wildflower,
Or in a blowing willow tree.

My poems were sad,
Or happy in words,
Filled with random, ridiculous thoughts
Of whatever a young girl's ears heard.

I'd fill my pages with nonsense,
About characters of fiction and wild tales.
But then my muse showed up and left,
And my fantastical stories feel so stale.

My muse showed up
In flannel and boots,
And Hallmark movies felt silly,
And Cinderella always lost her shoes.

My muse wasn't all happy endings,
But patient and kind—
Giving me space I so desperately needed,
Even if it meant leaving each other behind.

Days turned into weeks,
Weeks into months,
And every day I thought I couldn't breathe.
The idea of my muse was just enough.

I watched my words of color
Turn 1900s black and white,
And I realized the heroes in my stories
Couldn't always win their dragon fights.

My pages turned blank,
And I was desperate to know why.
The only ink I managed to roll out
Was smeared because I also cried.

I resolved myself then—
I could survive the last chapters instead of trying to thrive,
Resolved to meaningless words,
Because it was so hard to actually write.

Then my muse came back,
With boots and yellow flowers in hand.
And I swear music was somewhere in the background,
As before me my muse did stand.

I am a poet again,
Because my muse has returned.
I have rhyme and rhythm,
And my bottle of tears stirred.

Yellow flowers sit on my desk,
Right next to my ink and pen,
And a watch with a time
That connects a muse and writer again.

www.ingramcontent.com/pod-product-compliance
Lightning Source LLC
Chambersburg PA
CBHW060351050426
42449CB00011B/2929